How to draw Floral Mandala

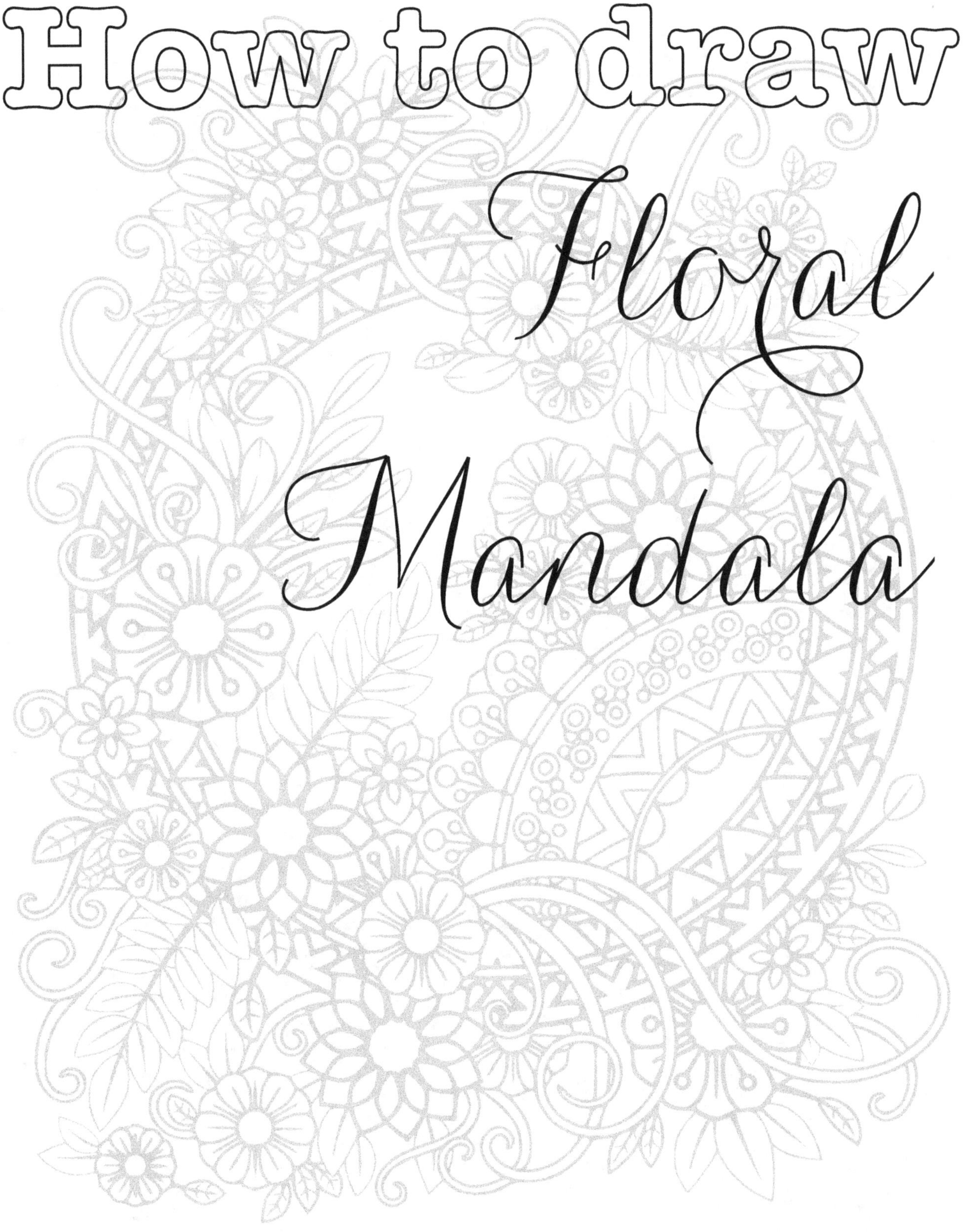

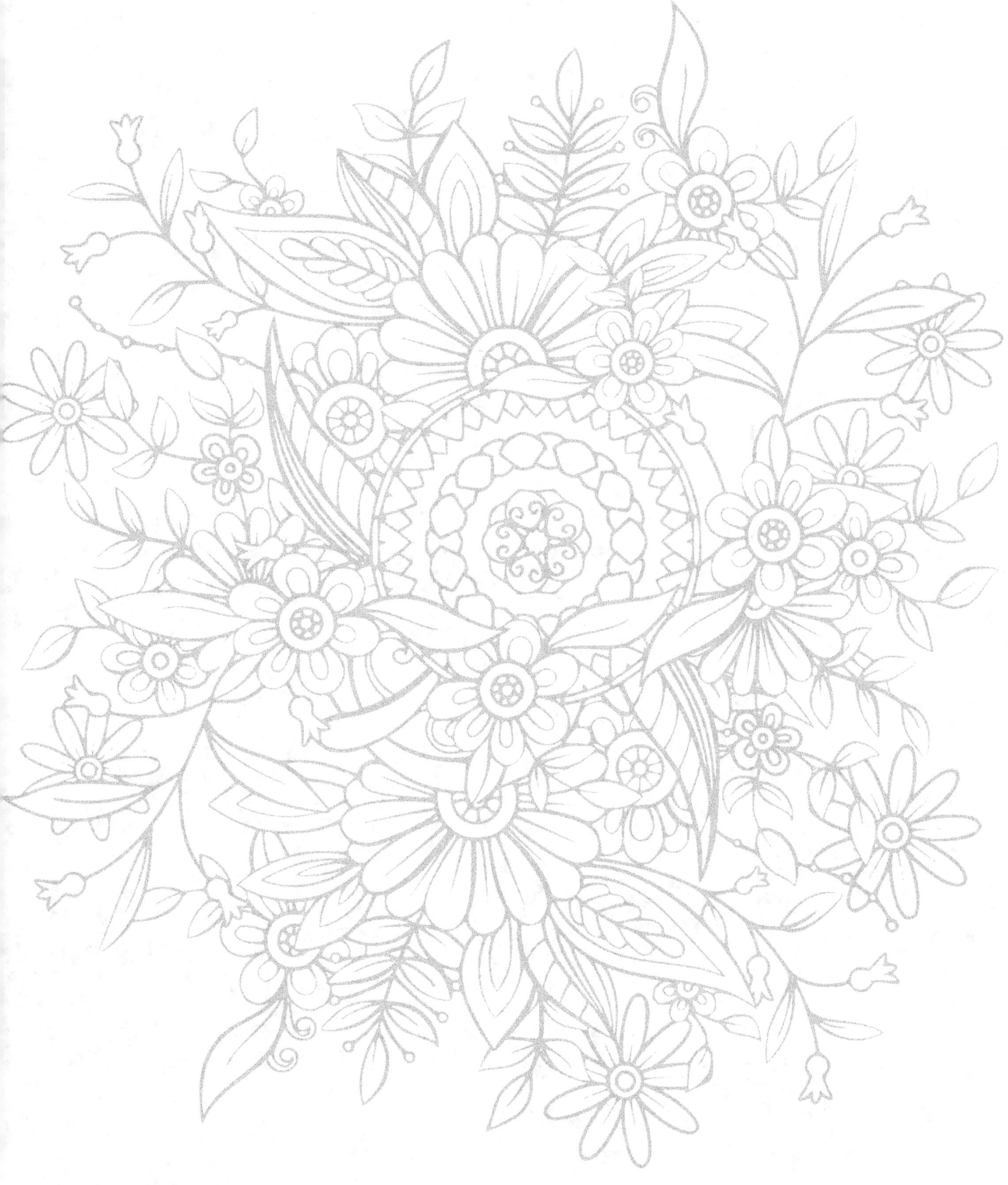

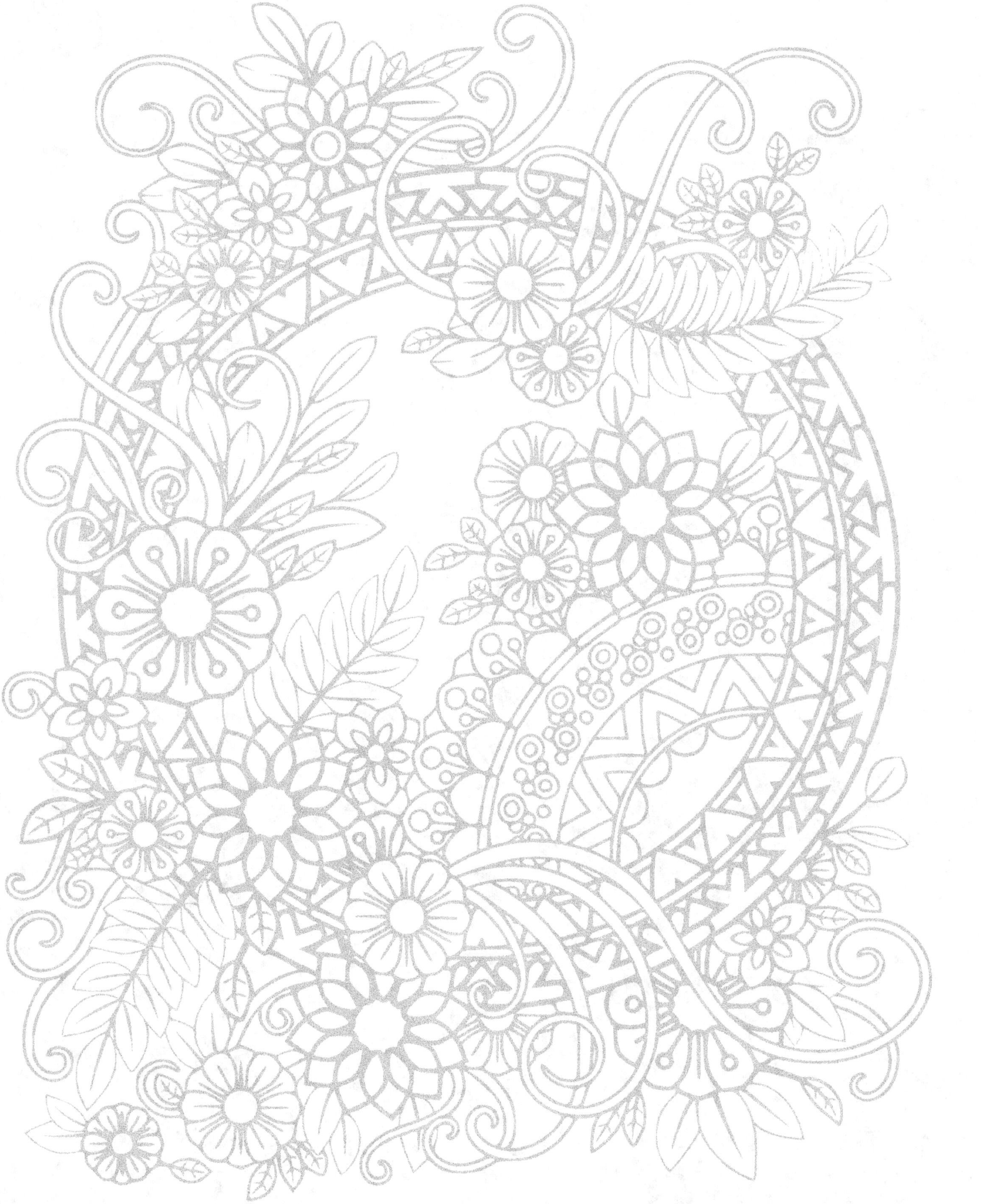

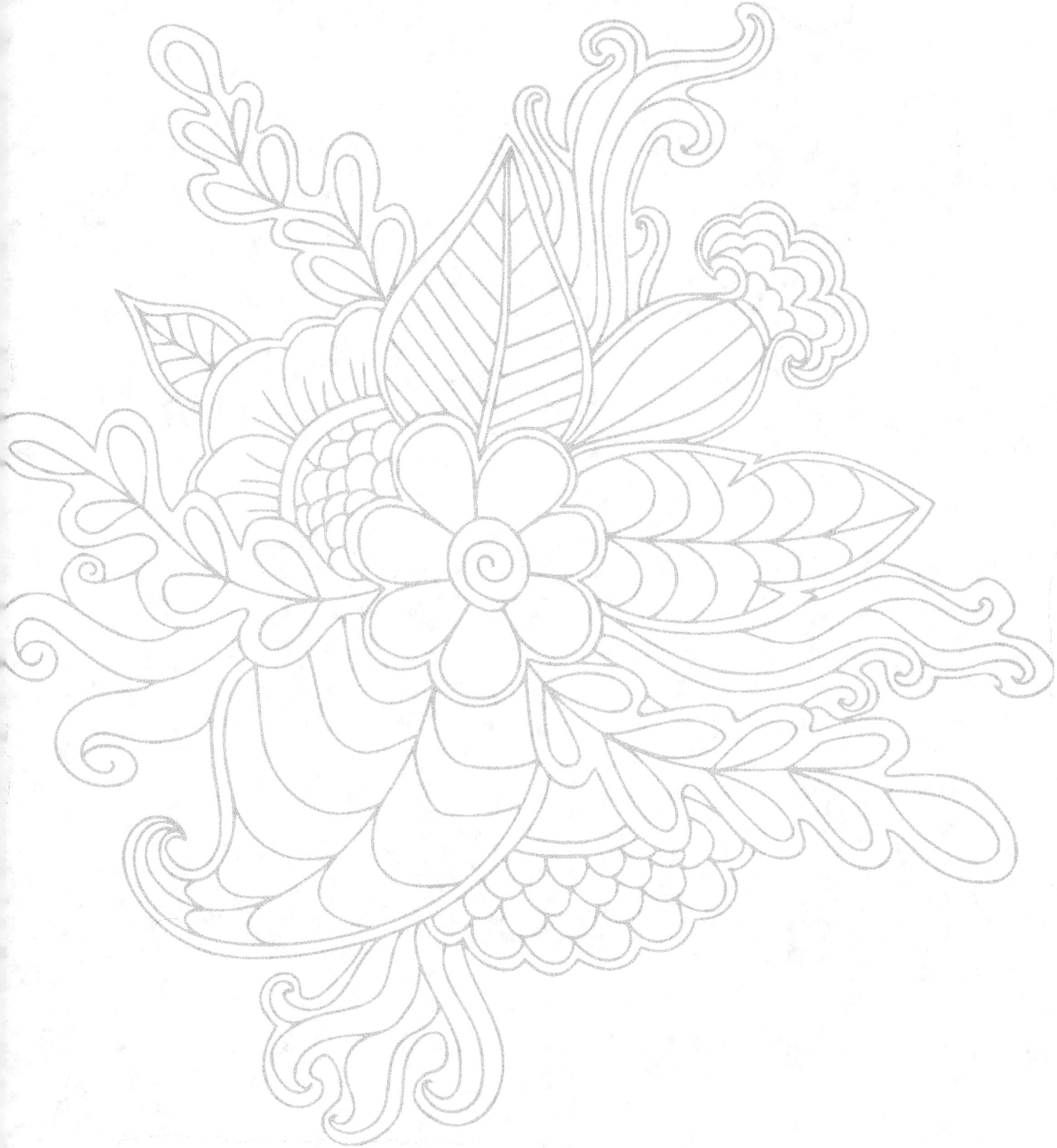

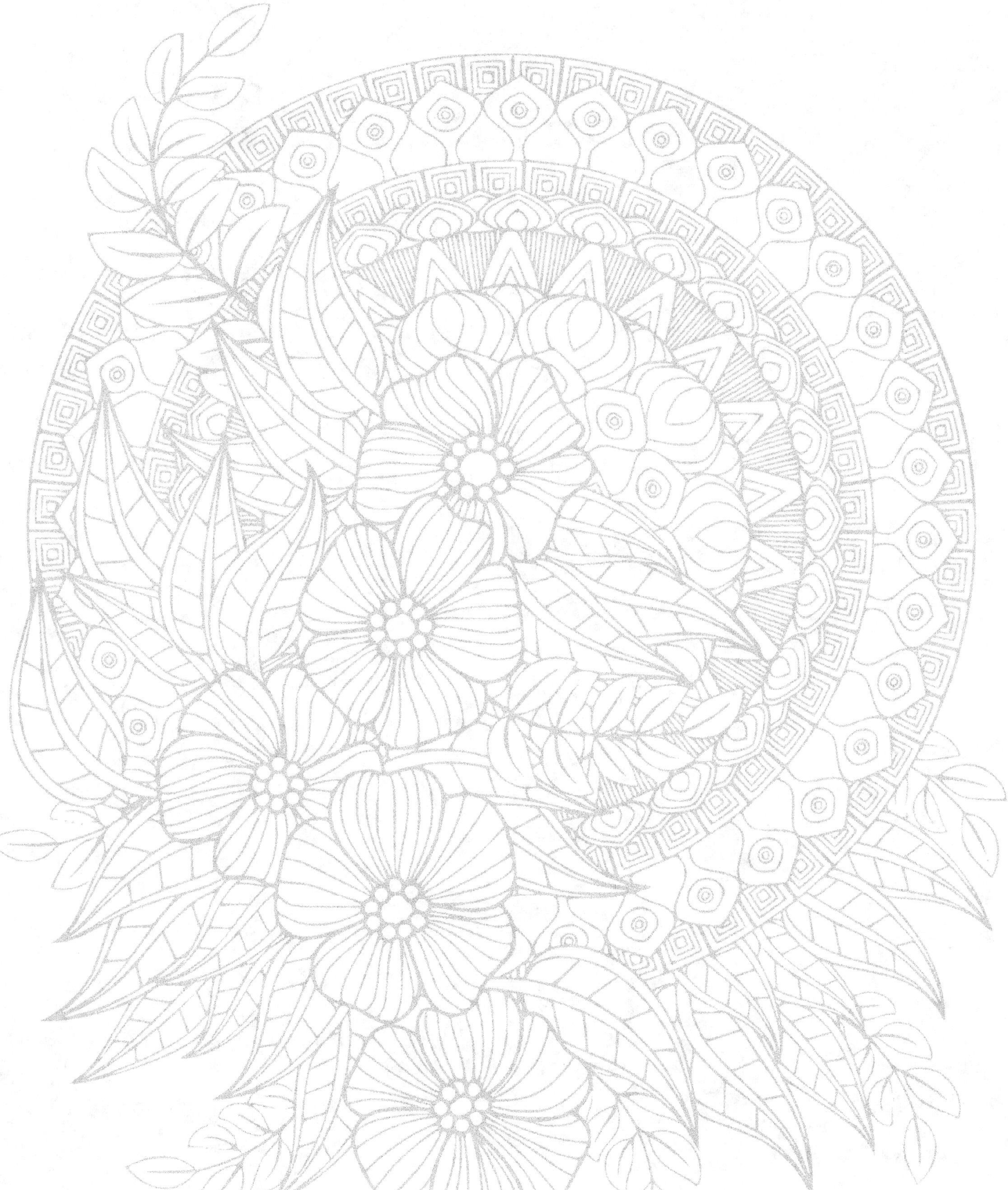

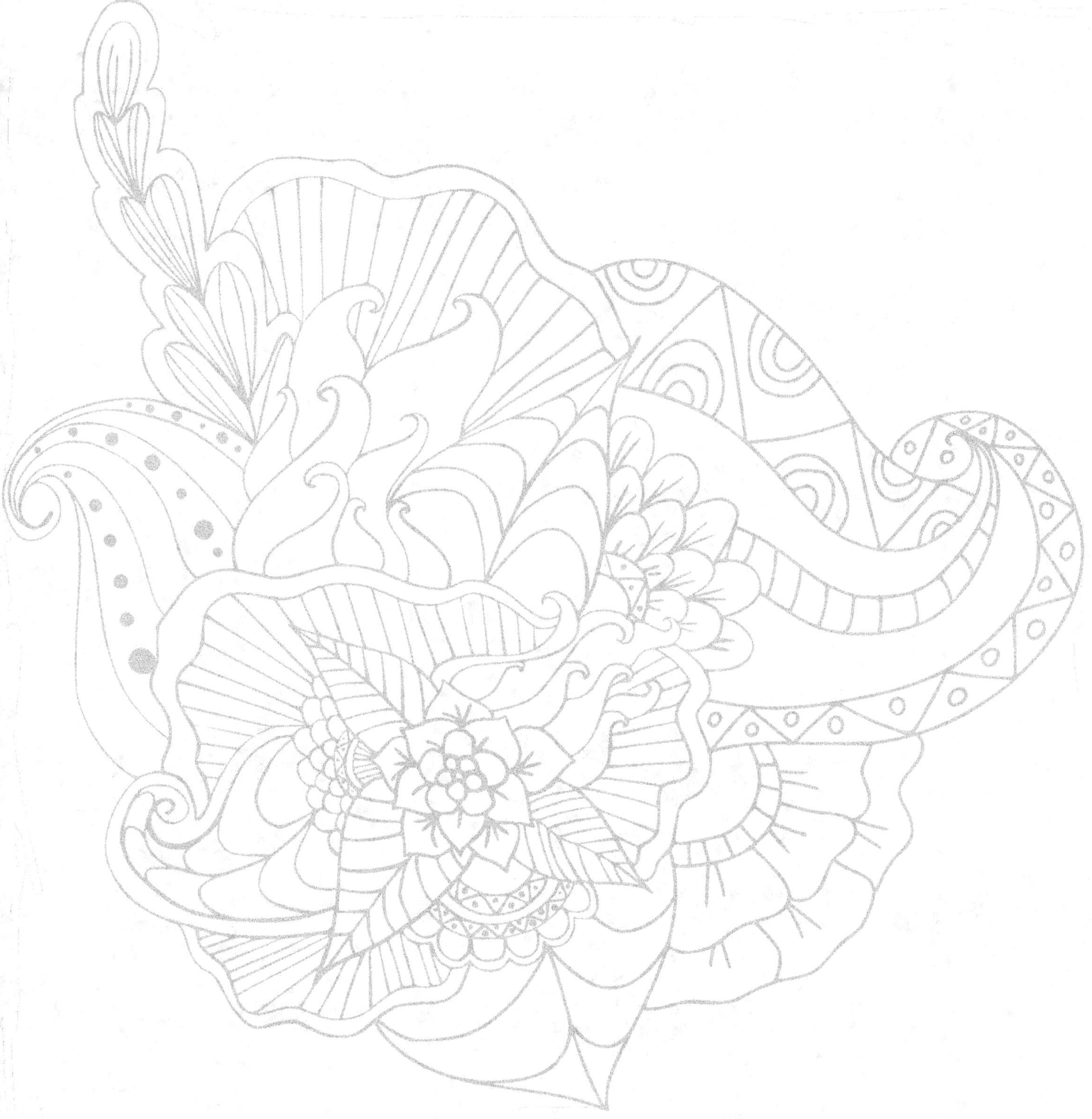

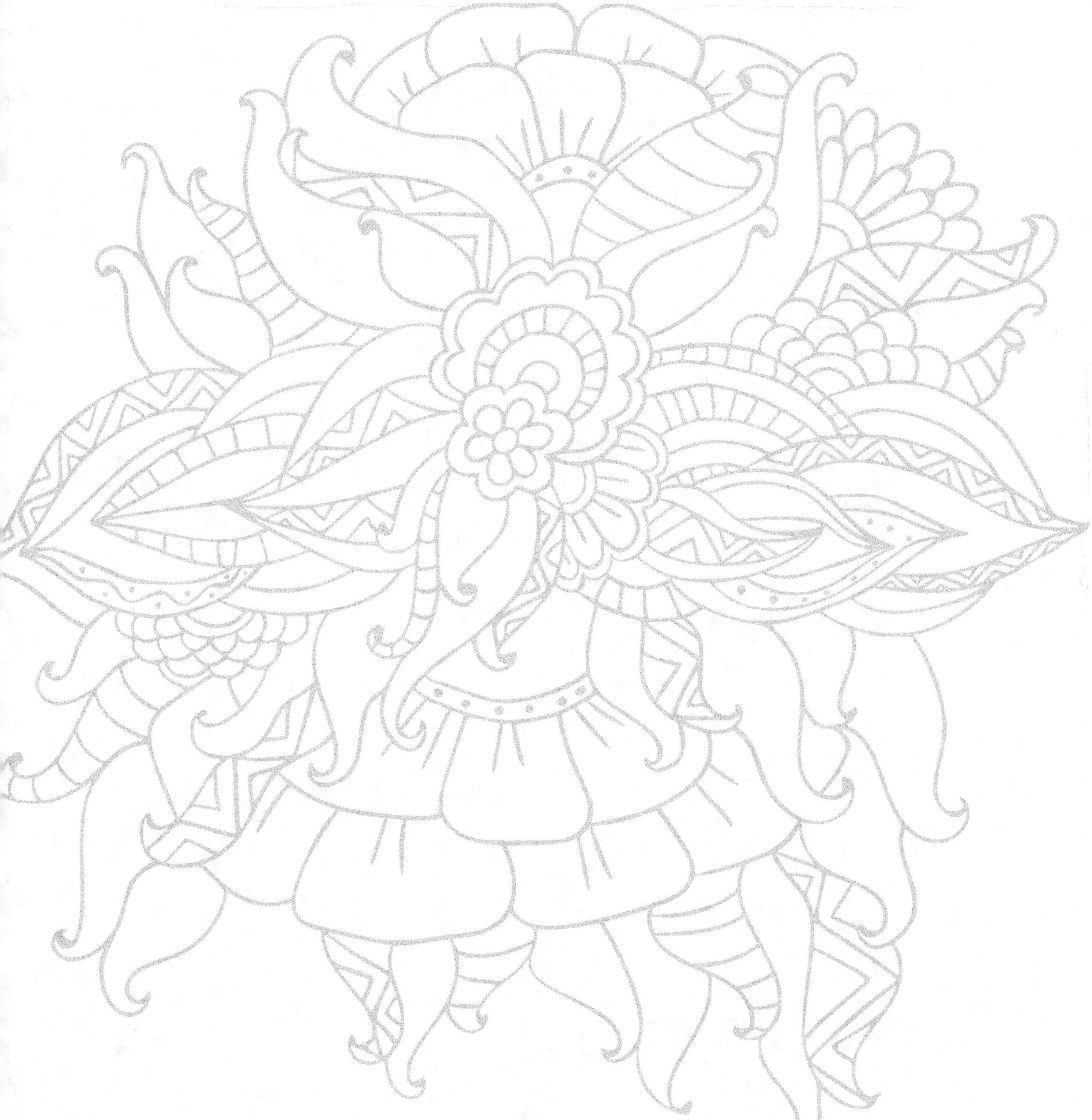

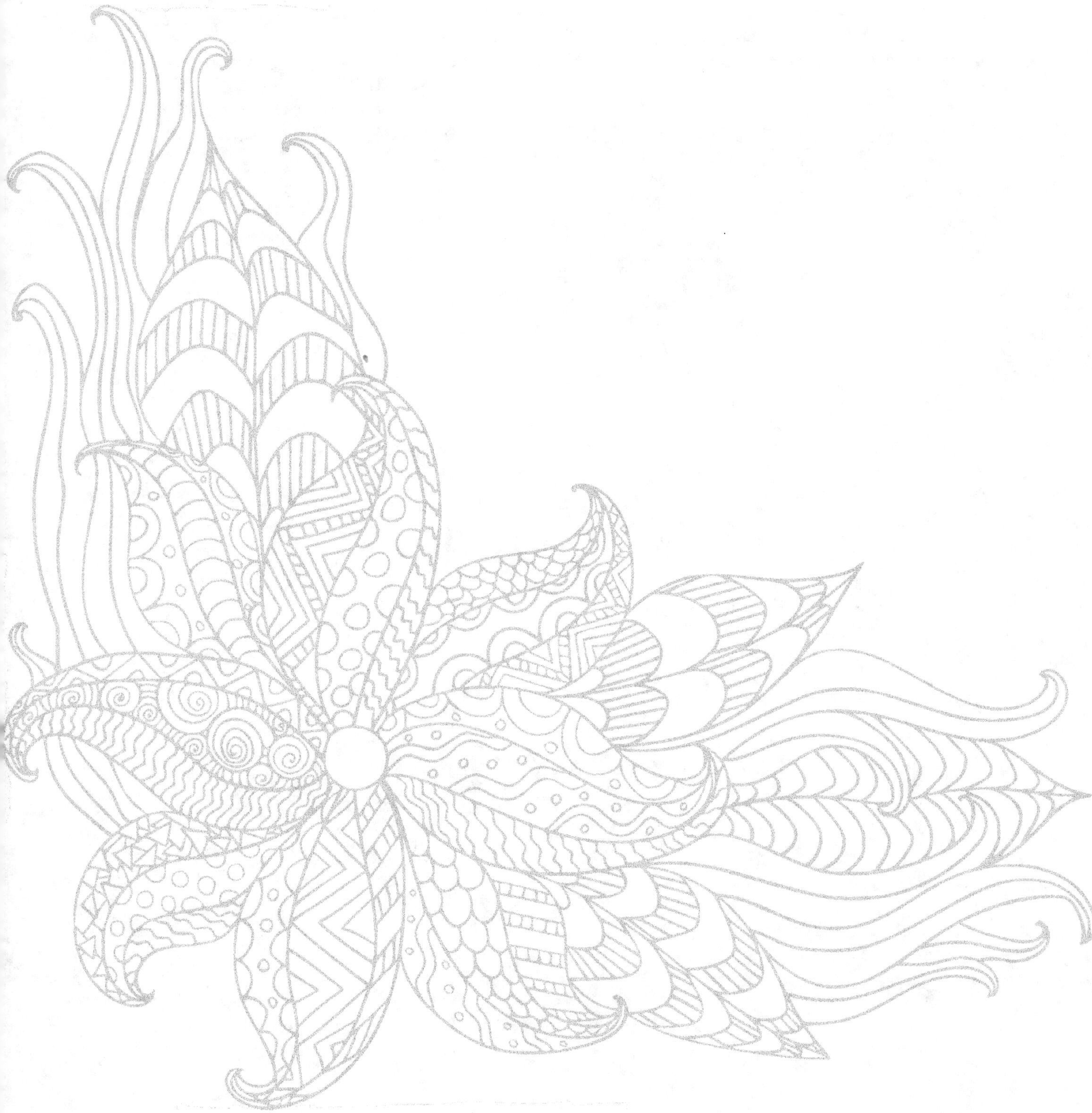

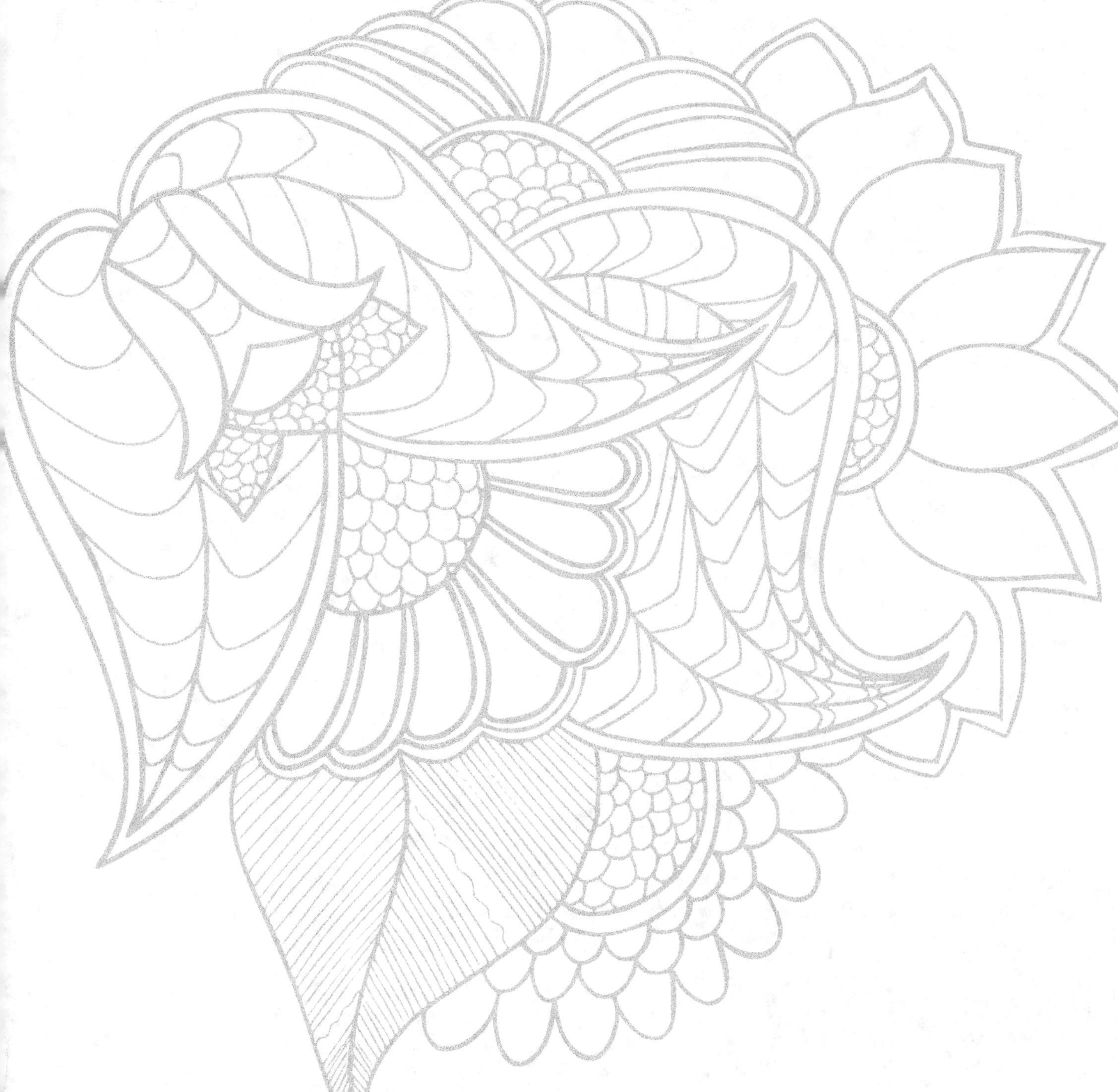

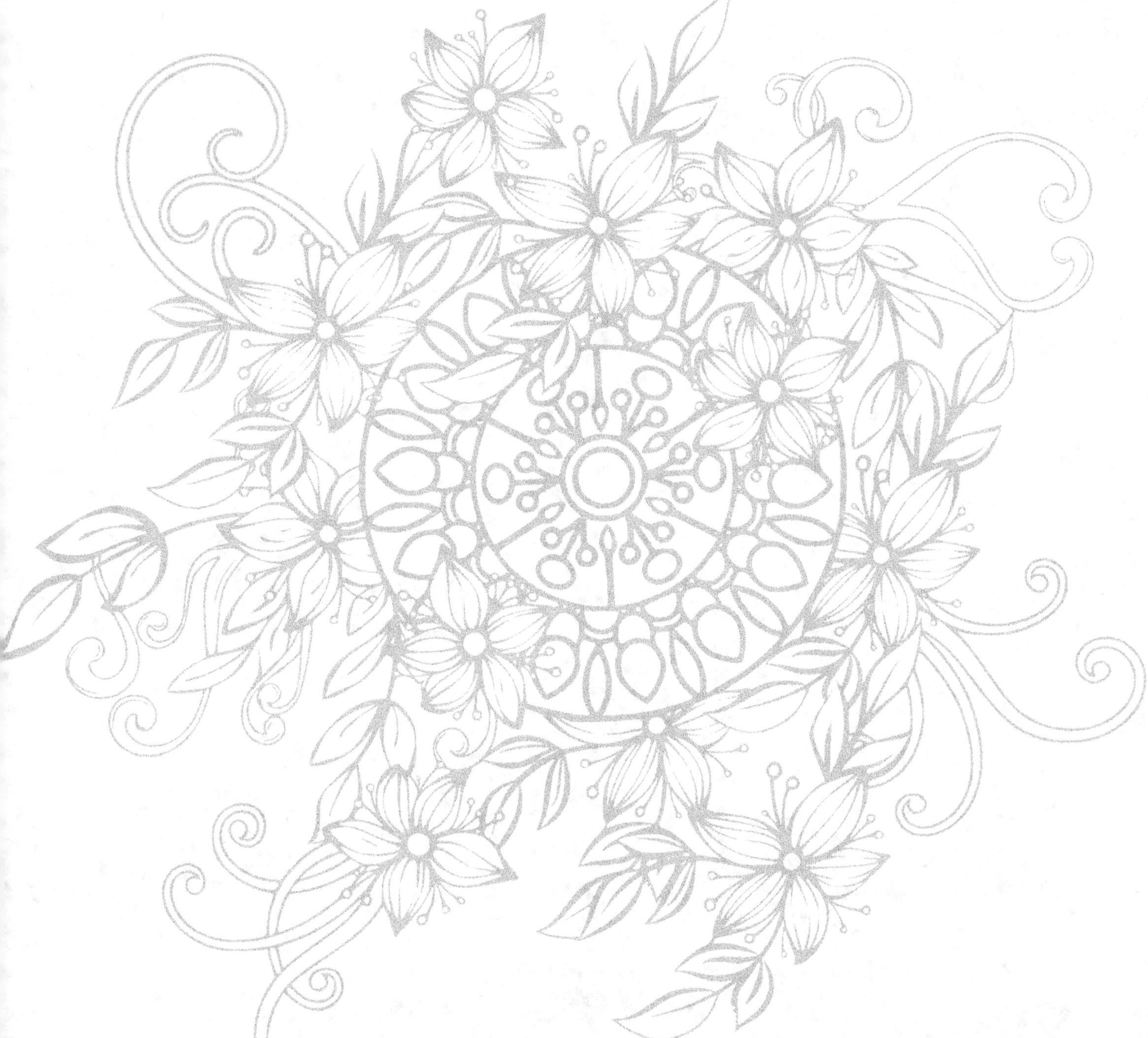

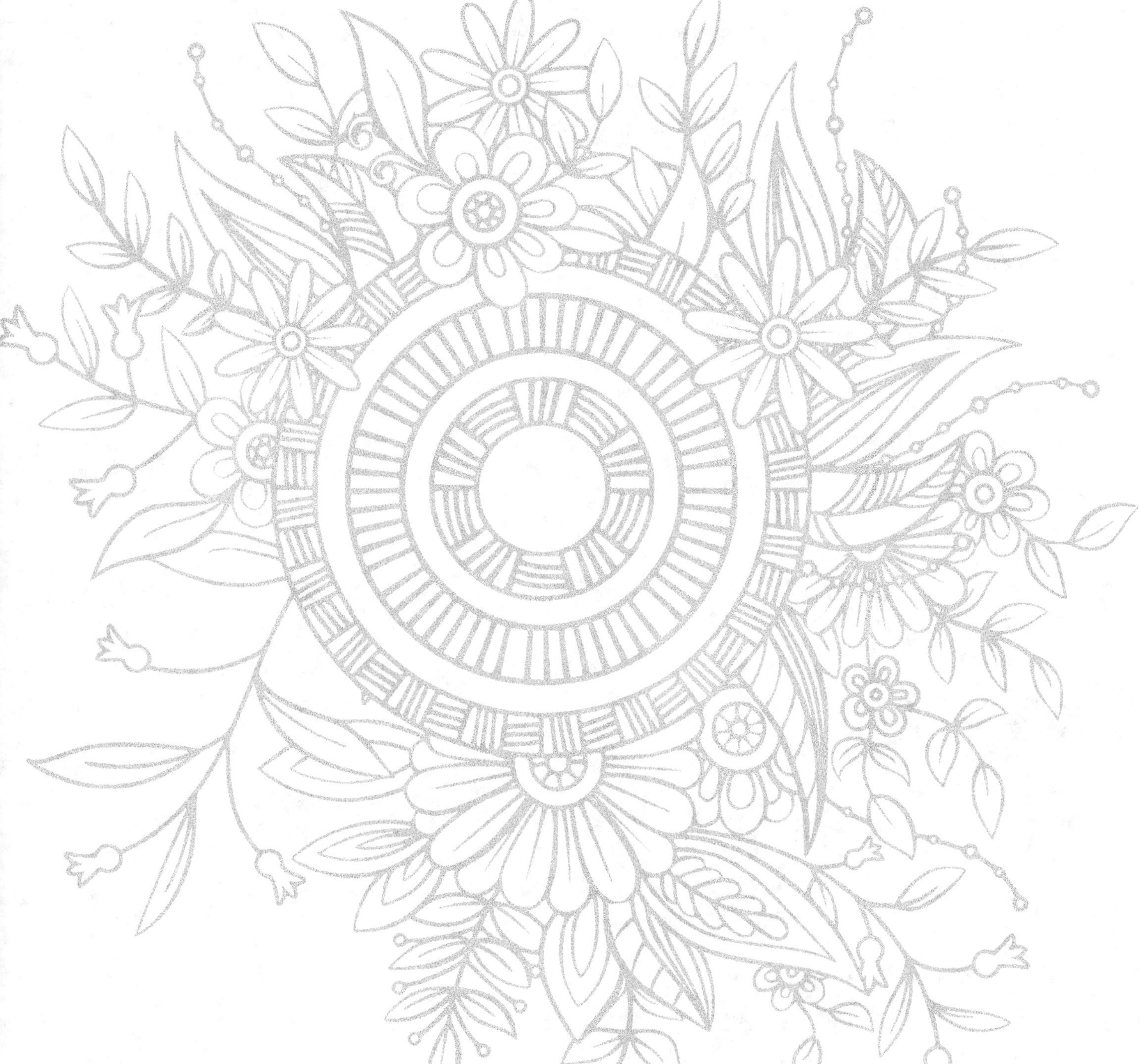

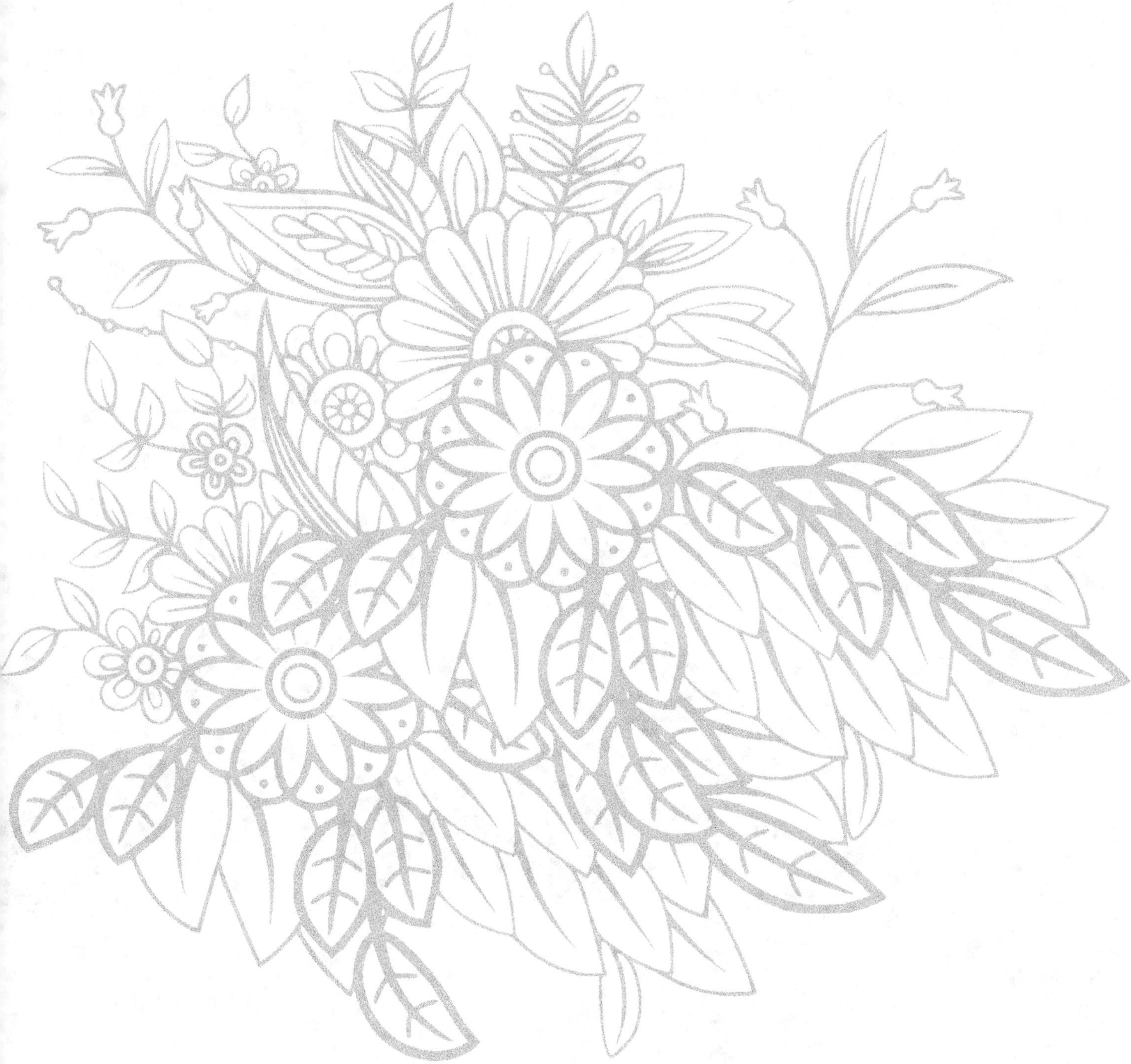

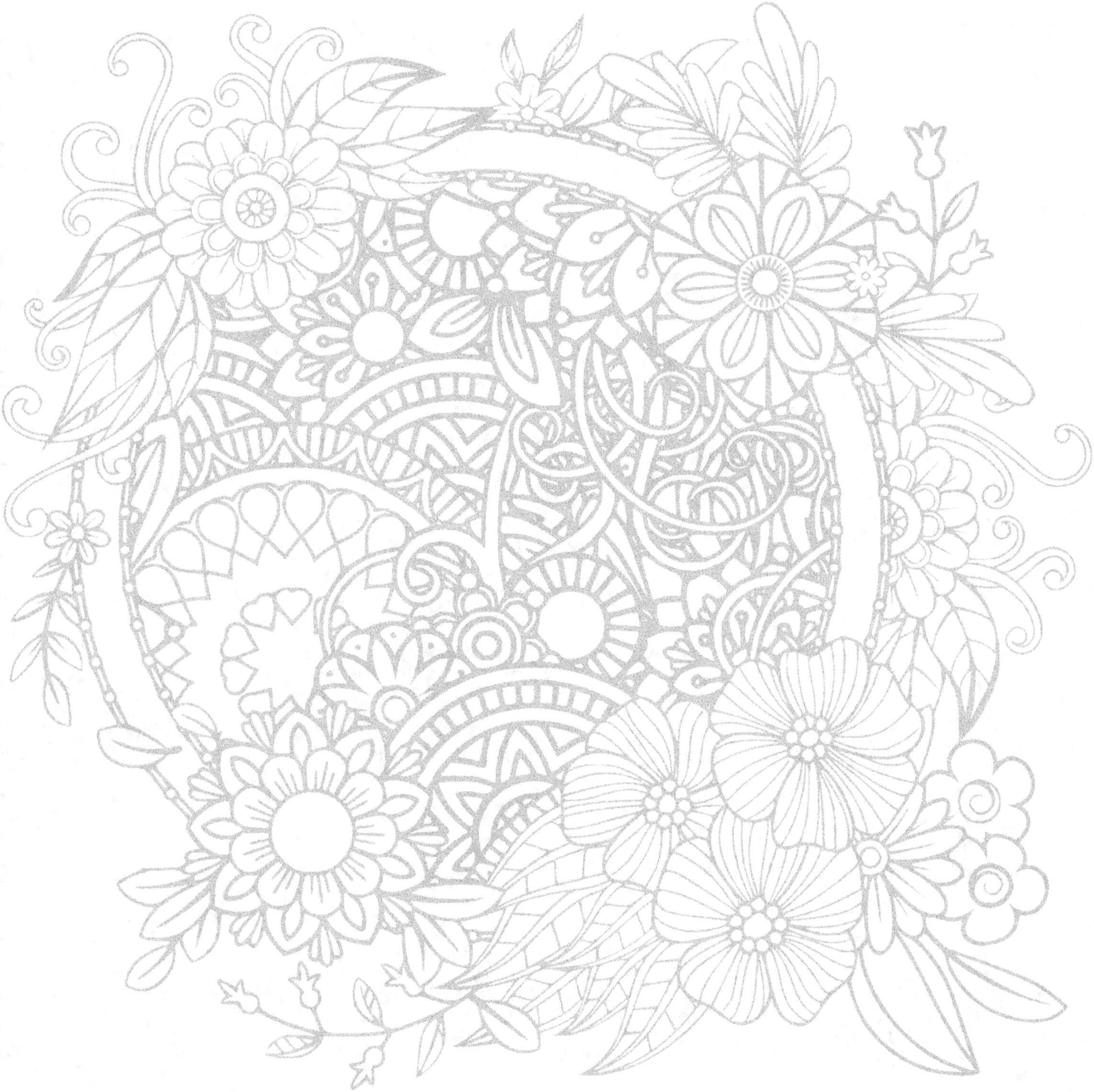

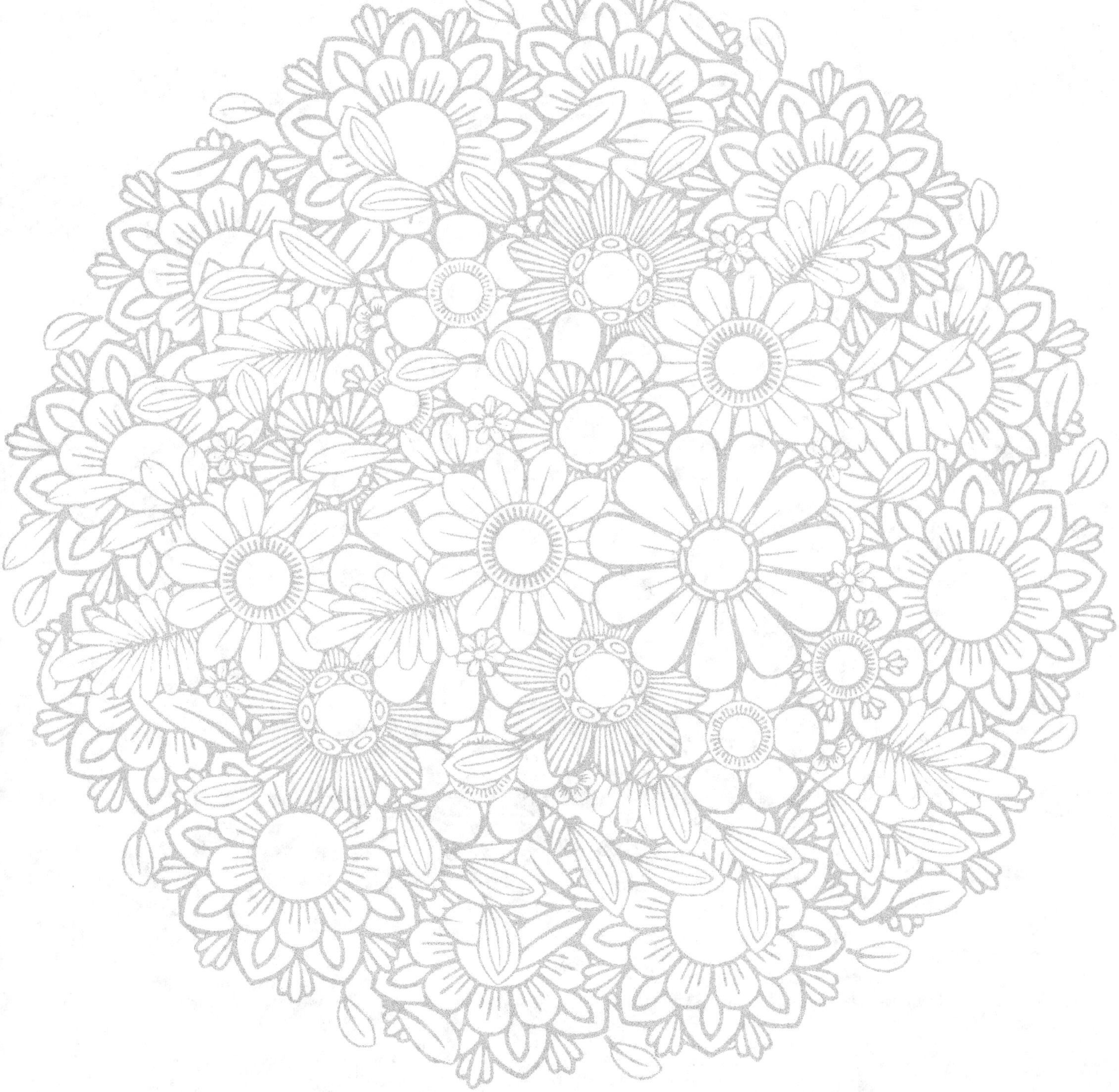

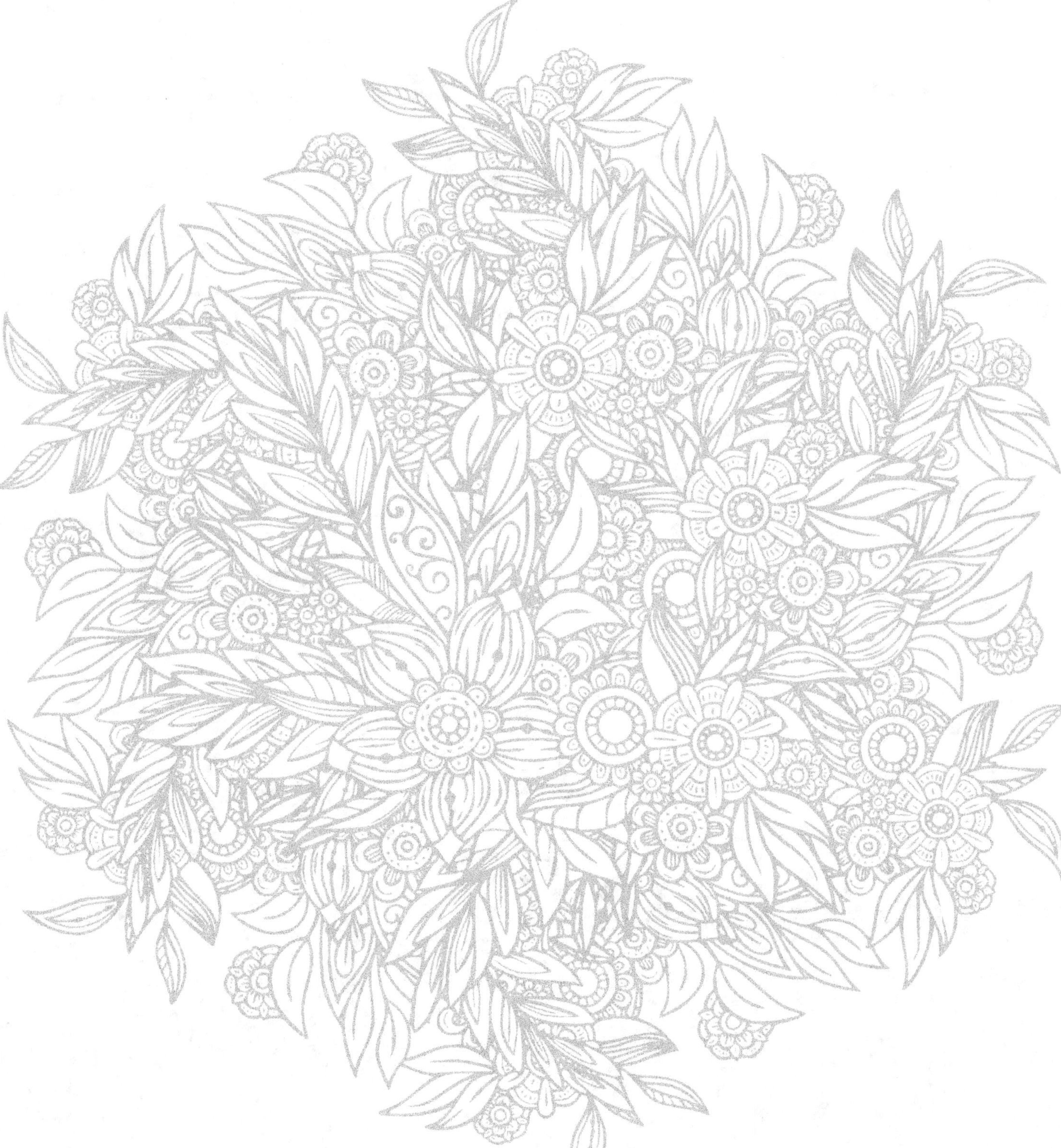

www.ingramcontent.com/pod-product-compliance
Lightning Source LLC
Chambersburg PA
CBHW081655220526
45466CB00009B/2769
* 9 7 8 1 6 5 5 0 1 2 6 4 8 *